I LOVE YOU

. . . .

HOWEVER YOU FEEL

For my Mum, with so much gratitude
for her unconditional love.

Published in Australia
by Loving Being Publishing
PO Box 256, Doreen, VIC 3754
marion@marionrose.net
www.marionrose.net

First published in Australia in 2025
Copyright © Marion Rose 2025

National Library of Australia Cataloguing-in-Publication entry

A catalogue record for this
book is available from the
National Library of Australia

ISBN: 978-0-6458575-7-3 (paperback)
ISBN: 978-0-6458575-5-9 (hardback)
ISBN: 978-0-6458575-6-6 (epub)

Cover layout, illustrations, and design by Marion Rose and Sophie White Design
Cover and back cover photo by Michael Rose
Typesetting by Sophie White Design - www.sophiewhite.com.au
Printed by Kindle Direct Publishing

Today, and every day, I acknowledge the Traditional Custodians of this land where I live and work, which include the Arakwal people, the Minjungbal people and the Widjabul people. I pay my respects to elders past, present and emerging. I acknowledge and recognise them as the original storytellers and wisdom keepers.

I'm so grateful to Aletha Solter, PhD, for creating Aware Parenting. I also so appreciate all the parents I've worked with as an Aware Parenting instructor since March 2005. Many thanks go to all the parents and children who were beta-readers and supporters of this book. Big love and appreciation to my extraordinary editor, Belynda Smith. I'm so grateful to the amazing Sophie White, who brought my designs into form, and my book publishing mentor, Julie Postance, without whom this book wouldn't be here. Thanks so much to Michael Rose for all his help with finding feeling words and for the photo on the front and back covers. So much love to Lana and Sunny, who taught me first hand about the beauty of being with all feelings. A big thank you to Alice and Luca for being willing for their photo to be on the front and back covers.

I Love You, However You Feel

An Aware Parenting book
for babies and children about
welcoming feelings

MARION ROSE, PHD

Hello, my lovely sweetheart!
I'm here with you. I'm listening.

I welcome all your feelings.
I love you, however you feel.

I love you when you're happy,

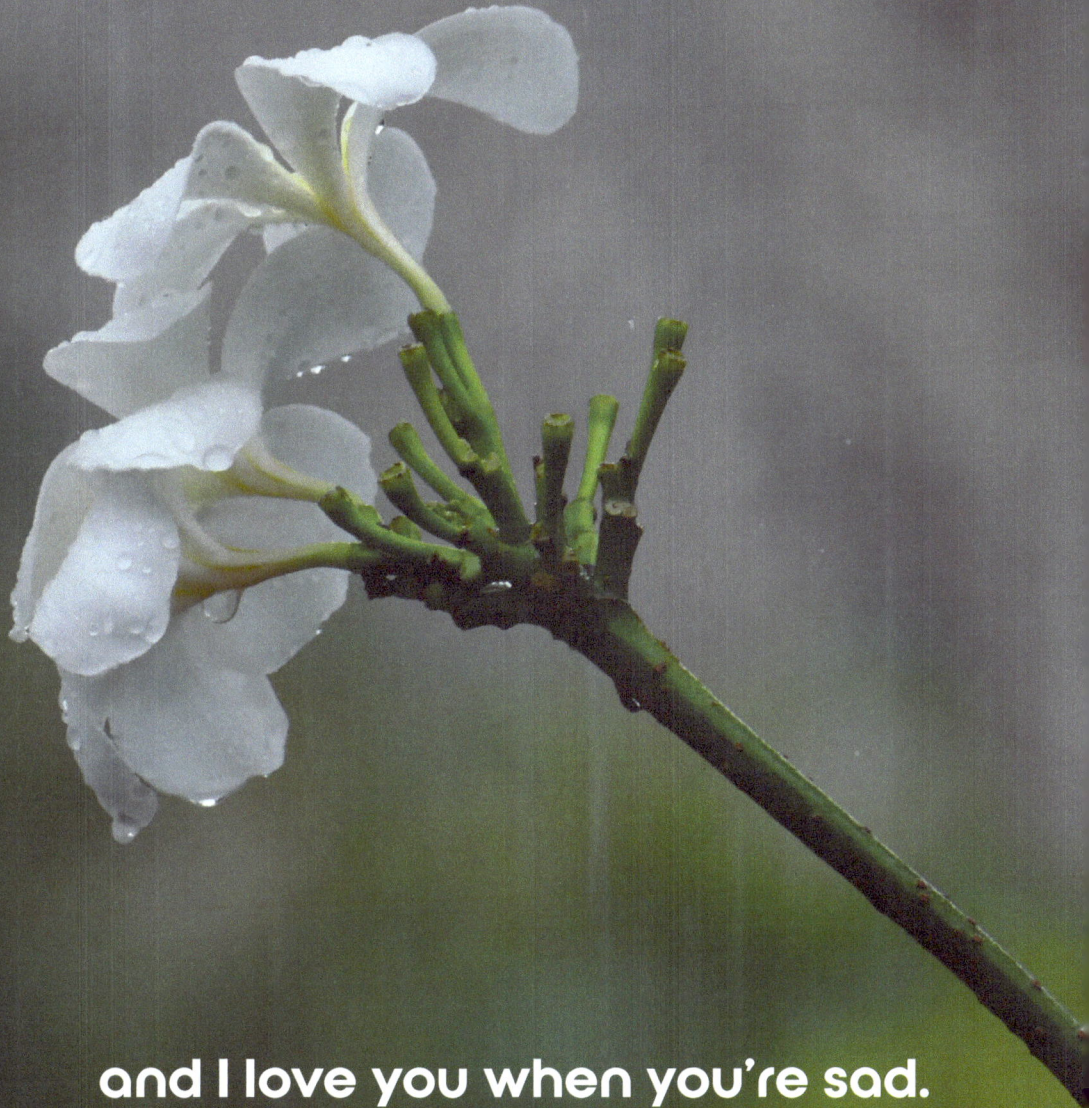

and I love you when you're sad.

I welcome ALL your feelings.

I love you, however you feel.

I love you when you're frustrated,

and I love you when you're excited.

I welcome ALL your feelings.

I love you, however you feel.

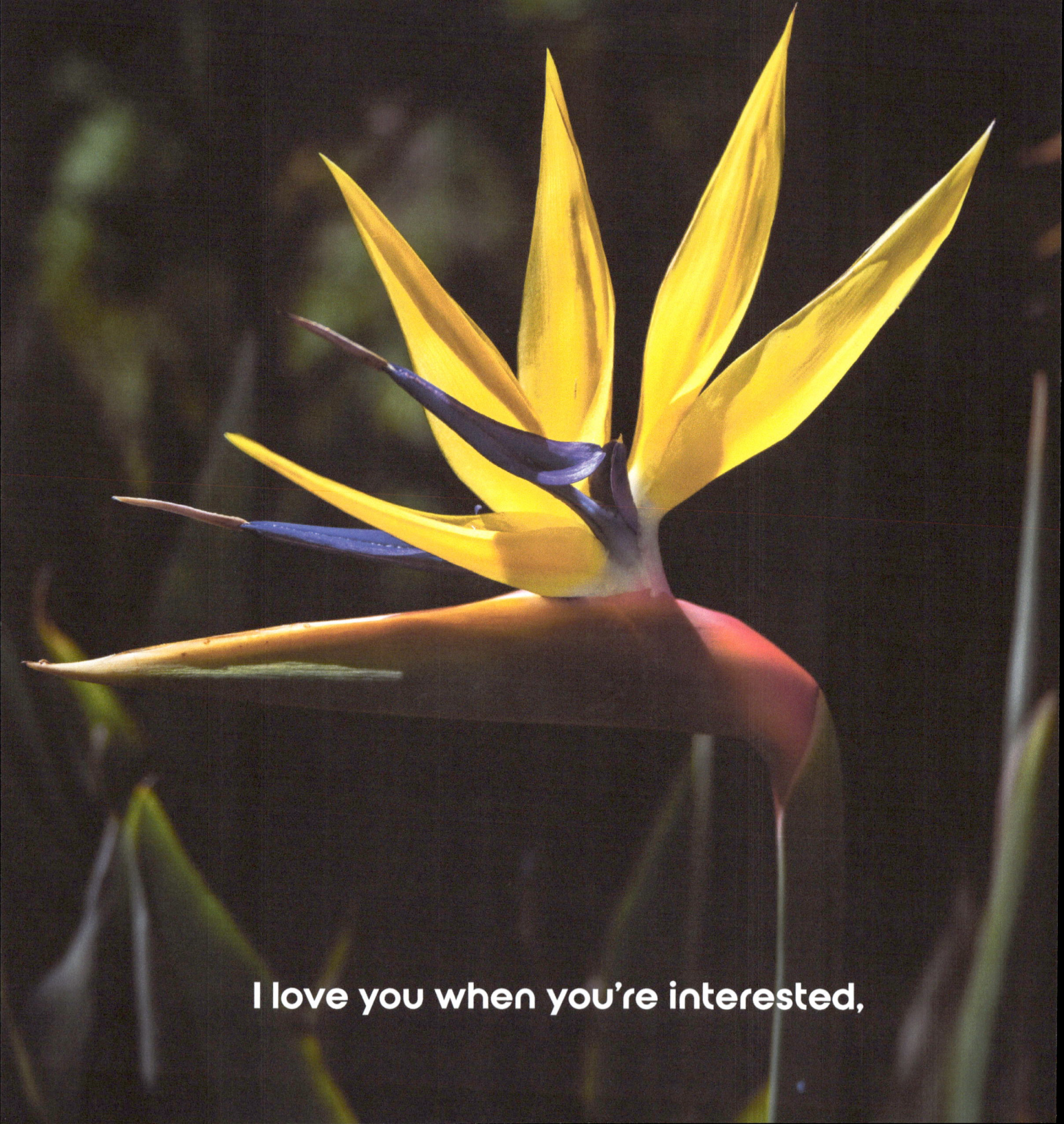

I love you when you're interested,

and I love you when you're overwhelmed.

I welcome ALL your feelings.

I love you, however you feel.

I love you when you're scared,

and I love you when you're confident.

I welcome ALL your feelings.

I love you, however you feel.

I love you when you're confused,

and I love you when you're clear.

I welcome ALL your feelings.

I love you, however you feel.

I love you when you're enthusiastic,

and I love you when you're unsure.

I welcome ALL your feelings.

I love you, however you feel.

I love you when you're relaxed,

and I love you when you're frozen.

I welcome ALL your feelings.

I love you, however you feel.

I love you when you're angry,

and I love you when you're loving.

I welcome ALL your feelings.

I love you, however you feel.

I love you when you're disappointed,

and I love you when you're delighted.

I welcome ALL your feelings.
I love you, however you feel.

I'm here with you, my sweetheart.
I hear you, I see you, I love you.
I welcome all your feelings.
I love you, however you feel.

Information for Parents

This book is based on Aware Parenting, the approach created by Aletha Solter, PhD. I am a Level Two Aware Parenting instructor and the Regional Coordinator for Australia, New Zealand, and Indonesia. In Aware Parenting, we recognise that it is normal and natural for all babies and children to experience a range of both painful and pleasant feelings, however much we aim to respond promptly to them and meet all of their needs.

Aware Parenting differentiates between two types of uncomfortable feelings. I call these needs-feelings and healing-feelings, although these are not official Aware Parenting terms. With needs-feelings, our role is to promptly attend to the need. The feelings will then dissipate, because they've done their job – which is to communicate the need. However, healing-feelings need to be expressed and heard. This is how babies and children release stress and tension caused by everyday events and any larger traumas, including birth trauma and early separation.

It is through expressing those feelings in our loving arms that babies heal from stress and trauma, which helps them feel more relaxed and present in their bodies. This expression can include crying and raging with our loving support. Expressing emotions also helps them sleep more restfully, concentrate more easily, and be naturally gentle.

Once babies are mobile, they don't necessarily need to be held in our arms for them to feel enough emotional safety for healing to happen through them expressing their uncomfortable feelings. Crying and raging are healing for children as long as we are offering them our loving support. When babies, toddlers, and children receive empathy and have their feelings heard, they are also likely to experience being unconditionally loved. They are less likely to need to suppress – or dissociate from – their feelings. This helps them feel more present, relaxed, and aware.

Please note: when we offer our unconditional love to a baby or child, it is natural that they might then share their uncomfortable feelings with us, or those feelings might intensify. This might happen after you read this book to the little one in your life. This shows that they are really feeling your loving presence. If this happens, you could speak the apt phrases to them. For example, if they start crying, and all their needs are met, you could say, "I love you when you're crying. I welcome all your feelings. I'm here and I'm listening."

It is also common that when children share their feelings with us, our own unheard feelings can bubble up. You might find that reading this book to the little one in your life might help your own emotions to emerge, especially if you didn't receive this kind of unconditional love for your feelings when you were a baby or child. Finding someone who can listen to us with empathy can help us feel a sense of calm and compassion when we listen to a child's emotions.

This book supports you to express your unconditional love to the child in your life. It also invites the child to connect in with the sensations they experience in their body when they feel particular feelings. Looking at the photos of the flowers alongside taking in the feeling words together can help the two of you to experience shared feeling states, which can bring about deep connection, empathy, and love.

If you want to learn more about Aware Parenting and how you can deeply understand the feelings of babies and children, both Aletha Solter and I have written a number of books. You might like to start with *The Aware Baby* or *Tears and Tantrums*, both by Aletha Solter, and *The Emotional Life of Babies* or *I'm Here and I'm Listening* by me.

You can find out more about my work, including my books, podcasts, and courses, here: **www.marionrose.net**

You can find about Aware Parenting and Aletha Solter PhD's work here: **www.awareparenting.com**